MODERN THOUGHTS

JERRY ULYSSE

ISBN: 978-0-578-21105-3 (sc)
ISBN: 978-0-578-21104-6 (hc)
ISBN: 978-0-578-21106-0 (e)

Library of Congress Control Number: 2019900848

Publisher name: Jerry Ulysse
Publisher address: 1040 NE 162nd St, North Miami Beach, Fl, 33162
Publisher phone: 786-553-5626
Legal name: Jerry Ulysse

Lulu Publishing Services rev. date: 04/17/2019

Contents

Behind the Ink

I guess you can say that's me, the guy who hasn't figured out exactly who he is. Maybe through my writing you'll be able to uncover a piece of me. Throughout my life, I've failed before I've succeeded. Let's hope that's not the case with this very first project of mine, *Modern Thoughts*. I've always thought more poems would be read if only those who don't have the patience to break down literature could understand what's being read without having to dive into their thought process much. So, I thought to myself, *How can I get deep without being complex?* Then again, I thought to myself, *How can I get deep without being too obvious?* While trying to find balance between the two, I found myself stuck wanting to please myself in both respects. That describes me pretty much: stuck. Everything I do never seems to be enough. I find myself wanting to do more just to fill everyone's void, and when that's not possible I feel a sense of failure. Can you imagine how many times I've failed? I mean, we can never help everybody, right? Yet there's something in me that feels like it's possible. The man behind the ink is more concerned with who you are and what needs you want fulfilled than he is concerned about himself. That's why these poems will be a collection of your personal experiences along with mine.

The First Night

I saw her hiding,
so I hid.
It was the only way
of isolating ourselves from the outside—
world, that is.
We connected with no intention,
two lonesome souls
trapped in an elevator;
as the elevator went down,
we elevated up in thoughts.
Our words mended
a bonding atmosphere—
stranger,
do we share common interest?
We found out soon,
as words escaped our tongues,
not so common but
appealing.
A night that ended suddenly begins again.
Her smile gave hope, so beautiful.
We toured the city
till comfort levels raised beyond bars.
For me, there was still uncertainty,
even with the smiles
through those eyes.

I could not sync her emotions with mine,
as our bodies
began to grow weak from an interesting night.
We set up for bed—
small couch—but she fell right into my body;
it felt so right. We slept through the night.
Was this enough?
Could she have been
wanting to feel my touch?
I cautioned myself physically,
explored her body mentally.
Temptation was defeated for now;
she was leaving, and all I was thinking was,
A great night could have been greater.
Here's my number: our hearts
knew we'd finish our true desires later.

Naked

Behind your makeup, there's a layer
of beauty screaming to be free.
Natural speaks: do you see me?
Oftentimes, it escapes into the night.
More often in the day.
It's the rare occasions that it fears,
'cause it knows it'll be covered away.
I met both in two different settings.
Makeup glowed in an elevator
    filled with dark hearts.
Natural took a swim, your beauty so bright;
the sun took a bow.

Behind your attitude, there's a piece
of you that ignited the peace in me,
a counterbalance to the flaws.
Your mind speaks: *Can you open me?*
Before my response can make a way,
you shut down instantly,
so I reach for your heart that's
covered with wants,
which I pierce with a blade
to provide it with needs.
Your barrier of insecurities blocks access
to new beginnings, because the past
trails along vividly.

Behind your flaws, there you go naked.
Without shooting for perfection,
you somehow ended up perfect.
Without shooting for the moon,
I still managed to gravitate toward
your space.
Without your guidance, I found myself
in you—
not physically, but mentally extracting
your flaws while naked.

Envy Does Us Wrong

People hate often.
They envy your way of life,
wishing to accomplish what you have—
a life brought to the light,
a life that you deserve.
The struggles never heard,
the results brought attention—
the kind that's not safe
from a person boiling from your success.
Someone close hiding their hate;
their emotions hide in your presence.
Sharing giggles, the laughs, soundly smirks
the snake with the venom,
waiting for your hurt.
A close friend plotting
on the life you've achieved
strikes you at the weakest moment,
wanting your struggles parallel to theirs,
seeking to take a life
they don't deserve.
Oh, how close can this friend be?
Is it she; is it he?

Who wants the life they misconceive?
The snake slithers well
on the life in which it dwells.
The friend with the venom,
the envy from hell—
that one whom you've helped
time and time again—
will grow closer to your heart
just to stab it in.
Envy, the invisible enemy—
envy will ruin friends.
Envy will ruin family.

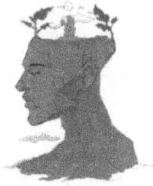

My Life, Your Entertainment

What am I, the president, that you
seek me so much?
Do I create excitement that your
life hasn't touched?
Am I the only star that you notice at night?
If so, would looking at me through a telescope
make you go blind?
I shine bright like wearing
loud colors at a fashion show,
getting attention from the tone, appearance
of my clothes.
Are you impressed by my jokes?
I'm such a comedian,
waiting for the next show just to
see me again.
Like the help of a tutor, do I help you succeed?
Or do I counsel your mind, make you
follow your dreams?
Sort of like a teacher, I cover my ground,
providing knowledge that happens to
keep you around.

Maybe I'm just your role model
wearing a suit and tie,
the entrepreneur guy whose expectations are high,
the therapist of your problems that
always get fixed.
Does that make me your hero? Does
my presence exist?
Do I get your attention
because I'm on the news,
The channel everyone tunes in to
before making moves?
Out into this world, broadcast me
on the radio.
Or google my information
just to watch me be exposed.
Every season changes weather
like every mood changes feelings.
Now really, does my life
seem to be appealing?
You watch; you listen.
This all makes sense.
It's obvious to see:
my life, your entertainment.

Finish Our Beginning

Should we finish what we started?
The thought seems so ironic
that we link up a trail which course
we never followed,
but still traveled the same distance
to cross paths again.
Down memory lane, our thoughts pile
the same wants,
but visions see a different life,
and both seem to be everything except right,
because it's not seeing you. An empty
portrait I must indeed pursue.

As I assemble thoughts, time doesn't
delay; every blink of an eye is point
seconds of my grasp for you slipping
away. So my eyes I'm afraid to close,
hoping to keep a tight grip of our bond.
Keep me close with no space to escape
as I inhale your exhale, the healthiest
air for my lungs; your breath airborne
through my system, leaving all nerves
numb. Yet I still feel empty—maybe
you're in, but not deep enough in me.

I sleep with your beauty, wake up with
your absence: is it a dream I'm chasing to
be real? Is there a connection my heart lacks
to feel? The signal's not strong; it's
been searching for long to connect our
feelings, but you've been so gone. Back you
appear, raising the bars in my heart,
'cause you place smiles that show many
meanings, say words that bring many
expressions, leave thoughts to have one
thinking one must finish what was started.

You Said

You speak from thoughts, ignoring the heart.
Reminiscing on the past,
you fled back to avoid a new start.
Moving on, the pain that strikes
wants not to be felt; any guy unworthy
tends to make the heart melt.
I'm the reaction
of words expressed through your mouth.
You wanted something new,
words uttered after emotional droughts.
A couple of dates here and there
gave me optimistic thoughts.
Was I the rebound?
Somehow, you let the ball drop.
Part of me feels like breathing.
I'm in the midst of asthma without a pump;
I'm in the midst of no circulation,
no oxygen for my lungs.
You invited me to your heart,
knowing the doors were closed;
you invited me to a place of emotions,
my key intended to host
where the truth never appeared,
where the lies stood tall,

with misguided information
converting a warm heart into a cold wall.
Caught up in my fear to lose your precious time—
a valuable possession—
while someone else held custody of your heart:
a valuable lesson.
The feeling of a fool is felt within,
ensuring it will remain
until my heart cures from this gloomy pain.
The persuasive act just felt so real;
the hidden lies were soon revealed.
Words you spoke will now be dead:
"I'm back with my ex," the last you said.

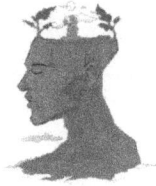

Lost Cops

Today, I woke up
and realized we aren't safe.
Our lost cops
have turned into murderers;
our protection
has turned into aggression,
the police neglecting their duties.
Yet every unit
voices that they're different.
By now, it's not the unit that's feared,
but the uniform itself.
If I call the cops today,
I might not see tomorrow.
But if I don't, guess what?
I might not see tomorrow.
There's a burglar in my apartment
has turned into me taking chances.
I can't trust any department.
It's not them all:
it's one phone call to one bad cop
who overextends his or her badge
to release one bad shot.

Once you make the call,
you go from victim to suspect.
Pulling up to the scene, they interrogate you—
something you never suspect.
Wait, what's happening?
I need your help,
and now that you're here,
I need more help.
Wait, I'm the one who called.
I just want this to end.
Put the gun down, Officer;
that's not what I meant.
Wait; I'm not being defiant—
just voicing myself
out of this hostile environment.
Wait, Officer, please—
you must be confused.
One hour later:
emergency room,
critical condition.
I'm on life support, all
because I tried to get some life support.

She Locks the Heart

Knock, knock.
Something's not right; we are
convicted for selling dreams without a price, left
finger empty. Wouldn't Jared be nice? Or maybe
Kay's the only key that'll leave a broken heart simply
amazed; at long term, we gaze. It takes a real man to
plan a wedding in days, a faithful man to make sure
the marriage never decays. Till then, the heart is locked. The
only key is commitment: locksmith won't get too far.

Knock, knock.
Locked yet easy to open.
Intelligent guys can't seem to focus, can only
go in hoping mission fails its purpose.
Approaching with a plan, seeming to cause more
damage, more complication for the next man, as
I go into work just as confused. This lock seems to
be hurt. Too much has tried, but entry declined,
her heart damaged from attempts,
yet so purified.

Knock, knock.
Let me in; don't let me out. Don't
be afraid; don't have any doubts. I'm the key with no
spare, around just one kind meant to fit your life. Meet
me halfway; don't leave me behind. Don't go on a run—
no tracking device. Don't make me hunt when you're already
in sight. I have the key. I have the key: numerous have
tried; they weren't me. I have the key,
so let me in. I have the key
this tragic ends.

Weird Friends

Your decisions
oppose mine the majority of time.
Opposites working together
never left me behind.
Even if you did, you always came back.
Had the worse arguments
but never lost track
of who we are, no matter
when times got rough.
When my heart fell short,
you stood alongside to resuscitate.
Times became reciprocal. I played my part.
As a friend with love,
I shielded your heart.
The moon and sun will never get along,
yet they both support earth—
never left it alone,
A dentist and a doctor
never worked the same charts,
yet they both manage to place
smiles on hearts.
The ocean and the beach

have been named apart,
yet they both can put out fire
before it starts.
You and I fight till our voices fade
Just to explain the same idea
in a different way.
Even though we seem opposite,
at the end we connect.
Even if we split apart,
I will never regret
The moments that we loved,
times that we hated,
the traveling experiences
that turned to debates.
Never agreed, but always
parallel to the same plan.
Like falling from two different planes,
on the same island we land.
No matter how much we fight,
the bond never ends,
the perfect description of
weird friends.

Selfish Love

Give me your love. Don't be selfish. I'm
the next after the ex, working
with pieces he left. It's difficult to
grasp while everything is being
held tight. In your presence you take
steps back to the past where
nothing was right, where nothing was fair.
I wasn't there, but through you
I see nothing but despair. Complete white flag,
you surrendered; you
gave it all you had. What's left you
kept to yourself, so weak.
Temporary pain can be healed with
a lifetime of love therapy, but
you're not attending my session, where
doors are only open for you—no repeated lessons.

Give me the pieces to a heart shattered
in so many sizes, a puzzle
for me to fix. Expect no surprises.
Give me your tears. I can wipe them.
Won't fall off your cheeks before I
dry them. Give me your voice.
I hear it. Venting's why I'm here. Speak, my
dearest. Give me your heart.
I won't break it. Just to feel it beat

close to my heart, I will tape it. Give me your
love. I won't hurt it. Find all
your hate and replace it. Give me your
life. I won't kill it. My purpose
is to fulfill it. Selfishness, don't embrace it.
Your heart, I will take it. I will
love it and create it to match mine.

Don't be selfish. Don't be selfish. There
will be no more past, only
future, no steps back as I pursue you,
no more darts stabbing your
heart, no more pieces shredded apart,
no more wounds to be healed,
no more hate to reveal, no more tears from
your eyes, no more pain, no more lies,
no more stress overnight perfect dreams by
your side, no more high-pitched sound—
yeah, the screaming gets too loud—
no more fights over
the phone, no more lonely nights at home,
no more calling friends
to whine about him 'cause you're mine.
No more him—yeah, that guy.
No more lust, only trust, in a life stored for us.

Mother Raised Me

Slaving in the kitchen, washing everybody's
dishes felt like punishment,
so I was always suspicious. Why me, only
age ten, doing so much work,
sweeping every spot in the house till my
legs began to hurt? Every time
I was finished, there came another task,
scraping tubs on my knees
like only I took baths, hot sun racking
the grass, the landscape job,
picking up leaves from naked trees
the seasons caused.
Acting out while at school. A phone call
to my house. She waited with a
belt in hand. "There's my handsome child.
Come here, my son. I received
a call. Here's a couple of words."
The belt hitting my skin
was the only voice I heard.
Why me?
I'm only ten, don't know any better.
Next day sitting in class,
suffering from after-pain of leather.

A lesson to be taught is a lesson
to be learned. Becoming a man from the lessons
taught is what I earned. From
slaving to discipline, I was always confused,
not realizing I was that special child,
not one being abused. When my mouth slipped
with words, she followed through
with a slap. I realize it was all love, not an
attack. When times became hard,
she made them worse.
I learned the strength
used under pressure is a real man's work.
I give her respect.
I give her my heart. I see things differently
only—and I mean only—because Mother raised me.

Three Days

Friday
was over before it started.
I caught eyes with the sun,
Shining in the dusk.
Yes, hot as she was,
I so needed this heat.
So I asked,
that her presence accompany me.
Her conversation let go steam,
Her body burning.
I'm talking skin so smooth,
lava couldn't damage her surface.
She danced so nice.
I'm sweating
trying to keep the rhythm right.

Saturday
I waited for the sun.
Instead came the rain.
Just by the way she sprinkled,
I knew it was a better gain.
She stormed to my presence.
Should I be on alert?
A beautiful scenery of lightning
as she struck me with her beauty.
Her eyes spiraled

an optimistic wave of energy.
She flooded me with drinks.
Low tolerance. I felt weak.
Let's not forget those lips
calling it tsunami.

Sunday
was dry,
no sun, no rain,
cloudy conditions.
Just like that she went missing.
I signaled out for connection.
We connected.
It lasted a second.
We attempted,
attempt, failed. Nothing but despair;
the memories
kept the hopes there.
I'm talking Friday lava,
the thought of her skin
flowing through my touch.
I'm talking Saturday lightning,
the only moment one could be struck.
I'm talking both days
combined
have done enough damage
to imprint my mind.

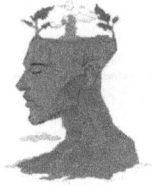

With This Little Life

With this little life,
you will become my light.
You will be the lamp distracting me
from sleeping at night.
If I turn you off,
I'm not strong enough to sustain the heat.
The beam from the light
strikes hard.
The electric current
makes me weak.
The bulb in due time loses power;
it dies out.
Reviving you only make times harder.
Hard times are usually
worth the trouble.
As my light,
you made me see things more clear,
A better vision the perfect tunnel.

With this little life,
you will be the hoarded mess.
While I clean my surroundings,
you'll be the only one left,
or placed in the bin with the rest.
But why put away something

I've worked hard to get?
So instead I shed light on your presence,
my only gift of clutter.
You may be the mess,
but it's mess I'm willing to clean.
Because with this little life,
you're all this hoarder needs.

With this little life
you will become my seed.
I will plant you in my heart,
have feelings grow from deep.
I'll have roots called feelings,
branches called emotions.
I'll have you,
my surviving water—
better yet, my entire ocean.
You will play a major role,
A spot that can't be filled.
Seeds will plant in one area,
and my heart is the spot you
revealed

with this little life.

Teach Me

Here I am in your presence,
ready to take the class.
My manners to love without fear
have vanished,
so I need your help to pass.
Teach me how to trust
when insecurities come around.
If I can't believe,
no relationship can be found.
Teach me how to think
without negative thoughts.
How can I be positive
if I haven't been taught?
Teach me how to communicate
when thoughts hinder my mind.
Because if I hold it in,
I might lose time.
Teach me how to listen
after witnessing false actions,
retaliating without a reason,
my emotions collapsing.
Teach me how to forgive.
Mistakes are commonly done.

We're all human.
I can't seem to forgive some.
Teach me how to share.
I'm being selfish with my heart.
It was fed lies once;
I'm afraid twice would tear it apart.
Teach me how to care
for passionate feelings.
Mine were taken for granted,
and I'm still healing.
Teach me how to become intimate,
to feel the love from your touch,
rather than only thinking foreplay
and nothing much.
Teach me how to surrender
without a fight
by making me realize
that no matter what my problems are,
you'll be in sight.
I'm going out of my way
just so you can see
that I can be a better man
if you're willing to teach me.

Who, What, When, Where, How, and Why

Who can I call when I'm feeling down?
I usually call you.
For now, you're never around.
What do I say when I'm lost for words?
A unique female
doesn't deserve to hear
what's already been heard.
When can I breathe if
you're taking my breath?
You're the gasp that I refuse to exhale;
I'll have nothing left.
Where can we go to distance
ourselves from the crowd?
I just want the sound of your voice;
everything else seems loud.
How can I run when you're my second leg?
We're attached as one.
So, if I run, you'll always be one step ahead.
Why should I walk?
Everything I want is in front of my eyes.
If I walk pass you,
another will take a shot, walking from behind.

Who can I call
when my thoughts are filled with sadness?
You're my usual smile.
Who will fulfill your absence?
What do I say
when so much is rushing through my mind at once?
You know when I'm filled with thoughts,
the relief I get from your soothing hug.
When can I breathe? We share the same lungs.
If you're not with me,
chances of circulation are cut, a man being hung.
Where can we go
to enjoy an adventure of our own,
create a unique idea,
travel through our time zone?
How can I run? I'm crippled,
one leg surviving alone.
The other gave out, disabled.
Why should I walk
if you're not walking with me?
no footprints, no sidewalks,
just a path that's empty.

Who, what, when, where, how, and why?

Where's Your Man?

You're single, which builds my curiosity.
Is it by option or choice?
Is it because guys are dogs
or because being alone is just something you enjoy?
Numerous questions
deserve various answers.
If I could read your heart,
figuring out the answers would end the chapter.
I realize it's not if guys can read the heart.
It's how we read the heart.
Understanding what's read
would be the best way to start.
What most men fail to see
is that not all women seek the same treatment.
Different women have different needs.
Only real men can see it.
Every woman hopes for a different person,
a character with special features
opposite from her ex who won't leave her hurting.
Fear is part of the reason
trusting guys can never rest.
You find yourself doing things
out of your character to help relieve stress.
While shielding your heart, you might

end up doing something you'll regret
by passing someone special
for the mismatch you've misread.
So maybe it's not them.
Maybe it's your decisions.
Maybe you have friends who give poor advice.
Toward the end you always listen.
Only a real woman
makes her own decision about a guy
when he speaks.
He speaks to you, and only through your eyes.
Maybe not every woman
Is meant to find that special person.
Even when he's found,
your past experience leaves you uncertain.
Now, sweetie, I must ask again.
Where's your man?
Maybe I can't find that answer
because I am your man.

Mistakes

Trouble comes, trouble goes.
We all make mistakes.
You're haunted by blame.
There's only so much you can take
before your heart emotionally breaks down.
While dwelling on regrets,
your soul cries tears.
Bad decision-making.
Your heart can never rest.
You've done something
that can no longer be taken back.
You try not to think.
Like a maze in your brain,
the thoughts are trapped.
To cover up your guilt,
we say mistakes are commonly done.
Seeming like everything is copasetic,
when sorrow is what we feel.
Not for what's done to another but,
instead, what's done to oneself.
It has collapsed your mind into depression.
The stress is quicksand to your health.
Learning to overcome a mistake

is like trying to overcome the guilt of fear.
It takes time to overcome.
Meanwhile, regretful tears.
If you face your mistakes,
you build good qualities,
become a better person,
which decreases the risk
of having your feelings.
as well as others, hurting.
People make mistakes,
reacting before they think,
causing them to do the unthinkable,
something regrettable
that makes reality sink.
It goes down the drain
and never comes up.
So, before you lose yourself,
hold tight.
Like steam in a coffee cup,
there's only so much guilt
and regret our hearts may take.
So before crashing down,
understand that we all make mistakes.

The Moment You Walked In

Excuse me, Miss.
May I grab your attention for a second?
You caught mine.
The least you could do is return the favor. Just listen.
I've been watching
you drink by the bar for a minute.
Instead of the drink,
I want to sip your heart, figure out what's in it.
You enticed my eyes
while amusing my thoughts with your appearance.
Never one at a loss for words,
you walked in—my brain froze—a moment of self-assurance.
So, everything spoken now
is coming directly from the heart.
You're appealing
in so many ways, I don't know where to start.
First,
I'd like to know if you're single or taken.
As I wait for the response,
my nerves tremble. Can you feel my heart shaking?
At this moment,
my immune system is getting weak,

afraid of rejection
while I'm eager to sweep you off your feet.
The response is you're single,
not looking, have been waiting
for the right moment.
So, I ask permission to exchange contact information
so we can grow to know each other,
maybe begin dating.
Right now
I can't offer you much but a piece of my mind.
If we exchange numbers,
set something up gradually,
I'll have more to offer in due time.
By the way,
you're really pretty, and I'm fond of your smile.
Is that a blush I'm seeing?
Thought I wouldn't get that for a while.
Glad
I took this approach.
Letting you walk out tonight in silence
would've built regrets within,
because you became my destiny
the moment you walked in.

This Blessing is Your Child

This blessing will make you scared,
place thoughts in your mind that's never there.
This blessing will make you cry,
a lake of worries dripping from your eyes.
This blessing will make you stress,
piling responsibilities that seem in excess.
This blessing will make you sick,
grow in your stomach, and begin to kick.
The blessing.

This blessing will bring pain,
ligaments stretching to create space for a new brain.
This blessing will bring smiles.
Nine months of torture becomes worthwhile.
This blessing will bring peace,
after months of growth, waiting to be released.
This blessing will bring life,
into a heart that's filled with excite.
The blessing.

This blessing will want love
from its carrier and the angels above.
This blessing will want rest,
to hear your heartbeat while lying on your chest.
This blessing will want food,
asking to be fed during its crankiest mood.
This blessing will want to be loud,
crying only because this blessing is your child.
The blessing.

Never See Me Again

"Stay out my life
and move on,"
the last words she said.
Those words pierced my heart,
almost left me dead.

My heart was bleeding,
chest flowing with blood,
being stabbed verbally
by a woman
I'll always love.

I stayed strong externally,
but internally I cried tears.
Losing the person
I fell in love with was
my biggest fear.

Nothing in life could
help me at this point in time.
Going our separate ways
was already in her mind.

She shouted, "Stay away from family.
Lose their number!"
They called at times for comfort.
For my humor they hungered

I'd promised in times of need,
no matter what, I'd be around.
So the thought became, *I lost one.*
Why let the rest down?

If I kept my distance,
every minute of my life
would turn to hope,
hoping to one day receive
the phone call.
The call will forever be
just a hope.

She stared me down.
Her eyes began to water.
It hurts when she cries.
The last thing I'd want is for her to erupt.

She hated me,
but our love was still stuck to her heart,
which made things hard,
because of me she wanted no part.

I've caused drama,
pain, and suffering in her life.
I've done horrendous acts,
which eat at me with regret
while I sleep through the nights.

I looked at her seeking mercy,
wanting her to forgive.
Slowly I took steps back,
looked deep,
and said, "Don't worry, 'cause you'll

never see me again."

Find Myself in You

It was love that once
carried me to happiness.
Little did I know, those legs
would fall short.
Soon I was dropped from the
best feeling to the worst.
My beauty wasn't enough.
My touch wasn't enough.
Eventually my love just wasn't enough,
or maybe it was too much.
Sigh, the confusion as to why
the little boy gave me a daughter
who's wondering where he hides.
Sigh, how can I explain
what's not understood,
the no-shows, the silent calls which
never spoke to ask if she was good.
Instead, I decided to find myself.
Who knew my hands
would be the biggest cure to my health?
I've kept us busy
by baking into her heart.
Mom, what's this? Mom, what's that?

Baby girl, it's just the start.
Let us bake our way to your first day
of school.
These hands will buy you clothes
with the lunch box that's cool.
Let us bake our way to your
birthdays to come.
These hands will support your growth
with a multitude of fun.
Let us bake our way through
every holiday.
These hands will wrap gifts
for you to open Christmas Day.
Let us bake, let us bake.
Let the worries escape.
For these hands have plans
far beyond the cakes.

Goodbye, My Friend

Memories will sink in till my
thoughts pile.
Walk a road full of sadness. Will
I walk many miles?
Who will pick me up along the side
as I journey by myself
through hopelessness?
My tears not to be wiped, instead
to flood the city,
to sweep the woman I once loved
like a depressed tsunami.
Goodbye, my friend, for there is
no looking back.
Neglected, my heart, the sadness throbbing
alongside a heart attack.
Today is not a happy day, nor will be
the days to come.
Every new morning will bring new questions,
and thoughts to sum.
Will the presence of next week,
month, or year exist?
Not to I, a ghost to the world, because
my heart is useless.

My evil deeds have come back to hunt.
My mistakes turned against me. This
position of lost hope, no man should want.
Goodbye, my friend. I've changed.
Could I have caused this much trouble?
Dreams and reality exchange.
Entitled to the flower itself, you became
my favorite rose.
The thought of putting you in a vase,
watering you, hoping our friendship would grow.
I guess not. Everything seems too late.
I'm walking down a lonely road with
lost thoughts, speechless, wanting to say
that you crushed my emotions with your
decision.
I'll love you till the end.
Nothing can be more painful
than having to say,
"Goodbye, my friend."

Time against Me

The more I want your presence,
the more I feel your absence
pulling away as seconds run your
schedule makes us almost impossible to happen.
Maybe I'm being too greedy.
For your company I starve.
The little time spent becomes a teasing appetizer.
I crave for more.
Time switches. One minute you're at work;
the next, out with friends.
A priority and cause for happiness
I would not interfere with,
still I deserve to squeeze myself in.
When things seem just right,
time plays a trick, keeping you in longer.
Through my ambition I wait patiently,
which makes my urge for you even stronger.
If I could steal your time,
it would be worth the crime
to rob you from sadness,
happiness the only evidence left behind.
I would leave a trace,

a special path for you to take,
hoping you can leave just in time
to join me on my sweet escape.
Time is against me,
so I make every second count,
writing cards and poems,
taking you to dinner then a movie.
Your happiness is paramount.
Whether it's once a week,
once a month, or once a year,
each visit will leave a million smiles and,
if I'm lucky, a million tears.
If I'm lucky,
time will expand, giving me open space
to kidnap you
for a vacation with amusement's trace.
Amused thoughts,
amusing experiences, just so you can see
I never gave up on making you happy,
even with time against me.

Trusting Guys

Trusting guys doesn't come easy at all.
The bond may either stay strong
or easily fall.
Trusting guys can lead to you crying.
They're great at first,
then they begin lying.
Like a lion turning its back
anytime it wants,
guys play with hearts
while searching new mates to hunt.
Trusting guys requires you to identify
the type you're dealing with,
one caught up in games
or one who's willing to shield
your heart with bricks.
Trusting guys requires you to trust yourself,
determining if you're making
the right decisions without help.
Trusting guys comes with intimidation,
with mixed emotions.
Will they be there through confusion?
You can only begin hoping.
Before you trust a guy,

ask if he trusts you,
the only way of creating
a moment of truth.
Trusting guys is a sacrifice,
one that can make you happy
or edge you along thin ice.
Every guy the same,
just processing different thoughts.
So, before you trust a guy,
understand the battles he's fought,
the damage done,
the ex who left him blind.
Trusting guys takes some knowledge.
Trusting guys takes some time,
but if you'll be patient,
the right guy you will find.

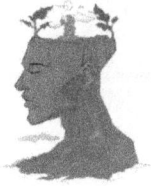

Today Affects Tomorrow

Today my heart was evicted from home,
left on the streets without shelter.
Now back on its own.
Today, if I dwell on my yesterday,
the possibility of taking steps forward
will decline.
However, how can I take steps forward
without her guiding me? I'm blind.
Today should I let it all crumble down this end,
when I have tomorrow to move on
and direct my heart to new beginnings?
Today for every start there's a finish,
and for every finish there's a start,
so I erase the past
and look for a better person to carry my heart.
Tomorrow maybe this person
won't carry my heart the same way,
maybe better, releasing hopelessness and stress,
knocking down the heartache.
Till then,
tomorrow like a baby attached to a pacifier

crying when no one's around.
I begin to miss our bond,
causing emotions to break down.
Tomorrow like a pool that has no water.
I'll feel empty, which causes sadness
to knock on my door harder.
Tomorrow like a road with no street signs.
I won't be stable,
and all activities will be done blind.
Today you ruined sympathy.
My heart you dismissed.
Tomorrow I'll make some changes.
Love to me no longer exists.

Hit On

Day in, day out, doors slam.
You're drenched, kneeled down,
swamped by tears.
You're scared, body trembling,
living love with fear.
Is that part of your beauty,
or is it a scar?
Are you in love, or
forced to pretend lust and wear scarves?
Being blind is a disability, but
you're making it an option.
Overpowered by low self-esteem,
you take abuse continuously
with no stopping.
The moment of pain
brings tears and shuts down your heart.
Suffering from his pessimistic ways.
Happy by day, abusive by dark.
Good morning. Sun comes out;
every activity in the sky can be seen.
Good night. Darkness falls.
You go blind.
Bruises aren't hard to see.
You know what's going on, sigh.
Can't seem to control your life.

The illusion of you being in love
is allowing abusive acts,
which is nothing nice.
The value of a shredded woman minimized.
In silence, you refuse to speak,
while your heart shouts,
Any male who hits a female
presents himself as weak,
while your heart shouts,
Don't let the head control the neck;
heads can't turn without permission.
So, you're his biggest threat,
while your heart shouts,
You're lost, misled. Please find the map
to help locate your sense.
Lying dormant in an empty place
from which there's no coming back,
you put your body up for grabs
to endure beatings, total failure for its use,
as you fail to recognize lust and
allow actions of abuse.
One day you'll wake up just before dawn
to eventually understand
women shouldn't be hit on.

Eighteenth Birthday

What about this day
that creates hype?
What about this day
that makes it seem right?
You become a special age
on a special day.
A special gift to your life
contributed in a special way.
This is your new beginning
to a legal life.
The day you dream of
when friends are out at night,
living the life of excitement.
When you're too young to join,
you hear about the fun,
while your patience gets annoyed.

What about this day
that brings out the smile?
What about this age
that makes it worthwhile?
The amount of love from important ones
touching the heart.
The number of places to which you can travel
without parents playing a part.
The presents you receive

from people who truly care.
The events you've once heard
that now you can truly share
with everybody else
who's dying to reach this age.
You become the narrator
of a life you've engaged.

What about this day
that makes the sky blue?
What about this age
that makes you feel new?
A blue sky turns into a beautiful piece.
A new age like a gift
becomes a rewarding treat.
The thought of no storms
showering your day.
The thought of your life
progressing away
shows that you're special
in every characteristic way
and even more special
on your eighteenth birthday.

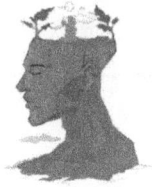

You Never Told Me

You never told me
that you would leave.
I'm clueless,
no heart,
lost deep in some sea,
waiting for a hand
that'll never reach out,
too weak to swim.
The disappointments
heavier than the water above.
The heart not pumping well,
traumatized from shock.
You took the fire from the torch.
It has no spark.
The thought of losing you
has damaged my mind.
No closure to move on,
left with no signs.
You never told me
you had second thoughts
about religious beliefs,
issues we'd eventually fought.
I just saw my queen,
the love before my eyes,

the beauty that flowed deep,
the beauty that hid lies.
Our bond had a course.
You veered away,
overwhelmed
by what family might say.
They took my life,
pressured indirectly.
You took my life,
followed them directly,
followed them to a place
your heart doesn't want and
left mine in a place
your heart will forever hunt.
When it realizes the
happiness just isn't there,
the missing piece
feels empty.
The feeling isn't fair.
And when you come back
to search for me,
into a new life that's carefree,
just remember,
you never told me.

if i Should Die

If I should die,
keep strong and focus.
Know that my mission
on this earth was accomplished
with God's purpose.
I took every breath that was allowed
in my time of presence.
Now I'm being taken
by an angel who shall
drop me off to a new beginning.
My time on this planet
was full of great experiences
and rough edges.
I walked through the rain,
ran through the storm.
Now I'm drying in heaven.
My work done was enough
to leave a trail of happiness.
So, at my funeral, everybody
look up in the sky,
blow my soul a kiss.

If I should die,
cry tears of happiness and joy.
Sink into all the great memories
we once together enjoyed.
Remember,
I lived up to every expectation.

So, when it's your turn
to run through the storm,
remember it's a common situation.
Only the strong survive;
the weak may trail behind.
Like going up a mountain,
the weak will think twice,
and the strong will climb.
I went up the mountain,
battled my fears,
and came back down,
which led me to being successful.
With my pride, I left proud.

If I should die,
remember my relationship
was with God.
We shared our secrets
during rough times,
and he led me on.
Our last secret was for him
to take me in his possession.
I had no more duties on earth,
so up I shall go,
where my soul will be resting.
Do me a favor at my funeral,
my loved ones:
try to smile and not cry.
Because, remember,
I'm in safe hands.

If I should die.

I'm So Far Gone

I'm so far gone into this
world of lust
filled with fake humans.
Whom can I trust?
When your world collapses,
Everyone turns their backs.
Those who were friends become
enemies.
Now I'm left alone the same way
I was born,
with no help, just responsibilities to
carry myself on.
So, I depart and go
far away
to seek research that offers lust,
a new meaning.

I'm so far gone into this
world of hate,
where love doesn't exist, hearts get
broken, shattered away,
everything fine goes wrong,
where the healing process
extends miles away
so the suffering lasts long.
Stuck between two options:

letting go or keeping faith.
The anger inside you explodes.
You become part of this world's hate.
So I depart myself and go
far away
to seek research that offers hate
a new meaning.

I'm so far gone into this
world of love
where happy people take vacations.
A paradise filled with magnetic hugs,
filled with real trust, healthy hearts,
and delighting smiles,
with everyone eager to help anyone
feeling down,
where there are always sunny mornings
with no stormy nights,
while everyone's personality symbolizes
a charming light.
So, I decide to stay on this
mission for long.
In this world I'm no longer
So far gone.

Stare Me Down Deep

When looking at me, you see a friend.
If you stare me down deep,
you'll see a guy who has you in mind
every second from within.
With you I see beauty.
I see sweetness
with a heart hidden deep.
You're inspiring.
You're appealing,
triggering my heart to skip beats.
As a friend you may see
that I'm helping you with problems.
If you stare me down deep,
you'll see me wanting to be your problems,
wanting to be the reason why you can't sleep,
not because your heart's broken.
Instead you met a guy so sweet.
As a friend you may see that
I'm doing you favors.
If you stare me down deep,
you'll see me wanting to be in your favor,
wanting to be that guy
to fill up your empty heart
with laughter and joy,

what you've always wanted from the start.
As a friend you may see
that I'm helping you with pain.
If you stare me down deep,
you'll see me wanting to share your pain.
Sharing what you feel emotionally
will make us one.
So, when I heal your heart,
mine is healed as well,
soul mates we become.
When you stare me down deep,
It's actually more than it seems.
When I stare you down deep,
I journey myself into this dream,
a dream that deserves no interruption.
As a friend I rarely show affection.
Your temptation weakens me,
sends me your direction.
You're all a guy can want.
You're all a guy may need.
If you stare me down deep,
you'll see for you
my heart will bleed.

Happy New Year

Happy New Year.
Physical distance so far, yet
heart so near.
We met yesterday; now
tomorrow's here.
The days may pass, but our
memories will last,
sinking, unforgettable
moments like an hourglass.
I took a road that
had no route.
Lost in your beauty, there's
no way out.
Lost in your smile,
which stretches
out for miles.
Lost in your words, which
silence those around.
I'm lost in your ways,
different directions each day.
Unpredictable
pattern to what seems to be a maze.
So confusing
yet unique.

A personality that's so
discreet.
A person everyone should
want to keep,
you possess what I want.
In search of
what I need.
Doors to your heart open a path
I may not see.
Your hallways are dark,
but this year
I'm walking through,
'cause it's the only way to
soul-search you.
Succeed or fail,
there's always a special
woman behind your
veil.

Can You Help Me?

Sometimes when sinking,
you don't know
whether to swim or drown.
When trying to fight water,
the panic takes you down.
When haven't studied for a test,
you don't know
whether to cheat or guess.
Both can result in you
receiving an F.
When dying from starvation,
you don't know
whether to buy or steal.
It's a week before you get paid.
You only have enough money
for one full meal.
When revolving your life around
one who leaves,
you don't know
when to rebuild yourself.
While stagnant, absorbing
the hurt from deep,
can you help me find myself
in times of confusion?
The deception
life carries while hurt,
my perfect illusion.

Sometimes you want everything
to yourself
but can't have it all.
I only want what's special,
the person who can
make my day
with every phone call.
What I have to offer is
less than what I want to offer.
So, I gamble my heart,
hoping to eventually win the heart
of someone's daughter.
Among the many disappointments,
bad regrets
haunt my dreams at night.
Help me not see past the present
when the moment has arrived.
It's like skipping school
and moving forward without progress.
I've been through the worst;
only happiness can dissolve it.
My empty heart filled
with cold winter longing below degrees,
I'm working with little patience,
seeking comfort. So,
can you help me?

Choices Make Us

The choices we make
show our character
attached to personality.
People make bad decisions
then refuse to face reality,
not accepting the fact
that they're wrong through it all.
We make an unconscious choice.
Pretty soon deeper we fall,
pointing fingers at others
for actions we plotted ourselves.
Once realizing we're at fault,
we look for protection
in some inner shell.
Because you're too perfect
to come out and admit
to your mistakes.
Making a couple of bad decisions.
The blame you're not
strong enough to take.
Sometimes pretending
to know it all can hurt you.
You become the leader
in choice making
when really you have no clue.
Or maybe the actions

were too much weight for you to hold.
Overwhelming mental collapse.
You're looking for an escape.
Better yet, you fold.
When really there's no escaping,
you only have the choice to fix,
thinking of the next step
to get out of the mix.
Making a bad choice
does not mean you're a bad person.
Not taking responsibility
for your choice will
only leave your character hurting.
Choices come from knowledge.
Choices come from liability.
Choices comes from confidence
with a positive personality.
Choices come from you.
Choices come from me.
Choices test our personae.
Choice is the key.
Like knowing where and when
to jump on the right bus.
Always keep in mind that
choices make us.

No Air

Someone help. A sudden pause.
Feels like you've stopped
my circulation.
My blood's not flowing.
I'm in total shock;
you left with no visitation.
Someone help. If I should pass,
it's because you stole my breath,
the thief with my oxygen.
Now I'm gasping for what's left.
Someone help. I know I'm drowning,
sinking in water too deep
with infected lungs, no respiration,
no angel to rescue me.
Someone help. Tell me how to breathe,
searching for lost air.
How does one inhale
what used to be, that which is no longer there?
Someone help. I'm breathing
from the inside just to stay alive.
This won't last long.
I need more to survive.
Someone help. My gravity, my gravity.
With you my world was stable.

My gravity, my gravity.
Emotions handicapped,
half of me disabled.
Someone help. The panic!
Somehow I'm still alive,
losing air by the minute.
What's left just won't die.
Someone help. The push
deep down, my soul inside.
The only sort of respiration
I have now is my pride.
Someone help. The search
with still no signs of you,
with still no signs of air.
Guess I'll be dying soon.
Someone help, someone help.
My final moments are here.
Someone help, someone help.
My destination is near.
You expected me to live
and breathe without you there,
the life that left me breathless.
My final gasp. *No air.*

She's Blind

She was never strong at heart,
carrying low self-esteem.
He broke her heart,
had sex with her friend
and snatched her back with ease.
She was mentally strong once, but
her emotions had the greater impact.
At the snap of the fingers,
he gave commands.
To his presence she's running back.
Some pursue to be naive;
she pursued to be dumb.
While she's laughing at the skeptics,
he's thinking what a fool she's become.
She's in jeopardy to unconscious attraction,
bad decisions over and over again.
Such his temporary toy for joy until
the new chick comes in.
Might be another friend,
might be another lost battle
from the temptation he blamed within.
A smile now turns into a cry later.
No wiping blind tears
when the heart breaks again.
She'll learn to lust.

Love then becomes her fear,
transformed into what she feared,
the breaking point for what was near.
Juggling between emotions,
she played with deceit
and couldn't seek the truth.
She always hated liars but
eventually became one too.
A sweetheart she was.
Her inner beauty stayed the same,
then her ex came around.
Within a split second her personality changed.
She's contaminated her character.
In my eyes still a friend,
she contaminated advice
by holding on to the lust
that led her while blind.

I'm Lost Without You

I'm lost, can't seem
to find directions.
Everywhere I direct my heart,
it signals rejections.
When directed to your route,
it begins to skip beats.
Leading straight back to you
without hesitation indeed.
During our time we've been through the best,
been through the worst.
Without insurance,
it came crashing down.
Deep down it hurts.
At this point I'm left to myself
without a helping hand.
As depression weakens me daily,
on my feet I no longer stand.
Some days I attempt
to carry a smile in my heart.
It turns into a sad face
when there's no happiness to start.
How can I gather myself
on a pace to move forward
when you're the only person
my mind seems to adore?

Tried draining my thoughts.
Like a plant, you're rooted in my cells.
The feelings for you are trapped
in me like prisoners in a cell.
Your presence distributes
optimism into my life.
Without that distribution
my personality is everything
opposite of nice,
distributing lies and feelings
with no strings attached,
giving women a clone
when you're the only one
who can bring the real back.
Some understand the principle
lost in the concept,
that you're the only woman
my heart acknowledges
and seems to accept.
I'm breaking the hearts of others,
not knowing what to do.
Realizing that nothing can be done
because I'm lost without you.

Fall Short

When trying your best,
time to time you end up falling short.
Some don't appreciate the effort,
so your presence they abort.
Trying your hardest at times,
it's never good enough.
Hoping everything will ease down
only seems to get tough.
Often still, you thrust yourself harder
to meet their expectations.
At the end all that's acquired
is negative feedback
with no character motivation.
Spending nights studying
for something that's not on a test,
not knowing until a packet opens,
being left with no choice
but to try your best.
Searching for misleading gaps
that may be causing you
to face disappointments.
When one gap is found, another opens.
Happiness for the moment.
Realizing the more you try,
the deeper you descend,
the phase of quicksand

like coming down a waterfall
then searching for dry land.
How can you make it to shore
if the waters pushing you back?
You swim with courage.
At the last second,
the strike from a rock
maneuvers your track.
That's why almost doesn't count.
It can never be complete.
You strive hard, then at the last minute
something sweeps you off your feet.
Babies fall short,
climbing back to their feet,
working hard for extra steps.
When perfecting the walk,
the times of shortfalls
are never something to regret.
You fall short to make a bigger move.
Only those with strong minds
realize falling short is something to pursue.
So, remember when you take one step back,
it's to build two steps forward.
When you take two steps forward,
it's because you learned from falling short.

Me against Time

It feels like I'm going against your time
and losing the fight.
Days are flying by.
The caterpillar turned into a butterfly,
still no sight.
I can only ask for so much
from a person of interest.
As the clock accelerates
with no response,
the ticktock inside begins hurting.
The thought of working around your schedule
created no moments for us.
When the grasp for time is mine,
other plans invade.
My solid hopes shattered into dust.
I guess a little of your time is too much.
Maybe none is what's preferred.
I'm attracted to you so much I refuse to see it.
Go blind until I'm for sure.
Your warm face
distracts me while time is running.
Your personality and glow
sparks up a torch,
keeps my heart burning.
You have become all I want to please,

all I want to see.
You have become all I think about,
spending nights in my dreams.
You keep me sweating,
confused, not knowing what to do.
Time's against me
when all I'm asking for is you.
How can one
beat this time battle I'm facing?
With you being so busy,
how can one
reach for the heart that
gravitates away, before it escapes?
I'm fighting for your time.
I'm fighting for your minutes.
Me against time,
one night to capture your heart
and everything in it.

Crushing on You

Crushing on you
is like preparing for a test,
hoping to make no mistakes
that'll land me in emotional distress.
If I think too hard,
I might overwhelm myself.
I relax my mind in hope
that my instincts come to help.
Like a test, if not prepared
to give you my all, I'll fail.
More pressure on the mind.
Nerves begin to drag me through hell.
Did I say the right words
or make the right decisions?
Butterflies eat me up
as the only emotions shown
are the ones I see with vision.
Your qualities may please
the sense of my mind.
Your beauty so appealing,
it can be seen by the blind.
You don't show much affection,
which makes me want you more.
Like a secret,
you hide everything,

playing hard to get, which I adore.
Words can only mean so much
unless they're shown out.
Set up a projector for my heart,
not the movement of my mouth.
I'm here for you as a friend
while holding on to this crush.
My heart throws a parade
each second you blush.
When you're sad it makes me sad—
you have no idea.
It's a crush that's hiding,
ruining our bond,
my biggest fear.
Waiting for the right moment.
Waiting for the right time.
If timed wrong,
I might not like the response I find.
You're the test that keeps me nervous,
and you have no clue
that I'm studying so hard
because I'm crushing on you.

Before Your Mistake

Manipulation to break
the line of respect isn't welcomed.
I seek equality,
a bond of mutual separation.
Her storm came by without shelter.
I embraced the flood.
The struggle, the survival,
they root from my blood.
The cheating I neglect.
The games, they get old.
No relationship with insecurities.
The emotions I control.
My pride beyond the clouds.
I settle for nothing.
She thinks she'll mess up
again. I settle for nothing.
If I allow the room for mistakes,
the disrespect was handed by me.
I understand the impact
of the past can drag a burden.
I understand it lasts.
The duration of the pain holds you uncertain.
We're human,
and I'm separated from perfection.

Some mistakes shouldn't be made.
We seek the wrong protection.
Regrets won't always be lessons,
instead a loss.
Stupidity the wrong investment.
How much did it cost?
If you thought before the mistake.
Your actions had purpose.
Pure ignorance.
The secrets eventually surface.
If you predict lust with no intentions of love,
it falls into your hands.
Sweaty palms drenched with guilt.
You played the wrong man.

i Can't Do This

I refuse to listen
to the negative thoughts
that hinder my mind.
Caught up
in your glow,
I made myself blind.
What I may want
is not what I'm ready to have.
How can I determine our future
while stuck on the past?
If I'm not honest now,
I'd feel guilty later.
As I end this now,
your feelings will hurt,
but view this as a favor.
I'm not ready
for commitment,
nor am I ready to settle down.
I'm hoping we stay friends
still share those moments we clowned.
I appreciate all you had to offer,
sense of humor and rational mind.
I understand this perception
of me leaving you behind.

I don't want you upset thinking
I'm a bad person.
The last thing I'd want
is to leave any female
uncertain.
If we're meant to be,
eventually things will fall in place.
Unfortunately,
at the moment, my priority isn't
commitment.
Speechless to say.
Maybe I shouldn't have started
something I wouldn't finish.
If we're both true,
our attachment won't diminish.
I tried to force something,
something that'll be missed.
I've come to realize, I can't do this.

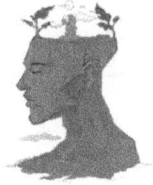

Watch Your Step

Looking up
before the journey, I noticed errors.
I noticed traps set to pull me back.
I won't let it be a terror.
During my first step, I ran into the streets,
where I was taught to steal.
Though the palms itched
I refused to let friends lead me into becoming a thief.
Then I began chilling with the environment.
Temptation every day built potential fights.
I remember violence
only created family visits to hospitals every night.
The influence of drugs,
the number one factor.
Turned it down once,
the end of the pure pressure chapter.
During the second step, I ran into school,
where my character in class
daily was to act a fool.
A class clown was what they called it.
Always thought I was just being me.
Eventually I stopped.
Mother was getting tired
of parent–teacher conference held every week.
Like the teacher, my energy
was for the students

waiting to be entertained in class.
Found out I was failing.
Damn, little did I know
those students wouldn't help me pass.
The grades were low.
For most dropping out,
would be the case.
A couple night school sessions helped out.
So, I walked across that stage.
During the final step, I ran into life,
where maturity is essential.
Deviate from wrong
to pursue what's right.
At the moment my future sleeps before me,
dreams of success.
College not so helpful,
the end of that tunnel shows promise.
I can't regress.
Direct myself to invest in knowledge.
Gain longevity of experience.
Multiply my gains
throughout the system.
Spread a virus filled with
wisdom, all because I took the right steps
to spread triumph.
And for myself have nothing left.

Understand Me

I can be the best at pickup lines.
When you approach,
the words fall behind.
I can walk on the ocean
without touching the water.
When walking to reach you,
I sink to the bottom.
I can sing a perfect melody
to entice many ears.
For you, my voice will panic.
Messing up is what I fear.
I can make smiles
stretch until cheeks begin to hurt.
With you
I may stutter through compliments,
so I halt before I flirt.

Let me be your guide through
crazy traffic, detour your
path where no dead ends happen.
Let me be the alarm
disrupting your perfect dream
with breakfast
at your side and napkins to keep
those lips clean.

Let me be the special guy you hate,
letting others break your heart
before taking it away.
Let me be tears
escaping your eyes,
running happily down your face
because I'm that guy.

Don't judge the water
for being cold.
Let the temperature
of your body heat unfold.
Don't judge life
while it's confused.
Fit into this world
where parts will amuse.
Don't judge actions to my scene.
Besides the scripts,
there's a better me.
Don't judge my heart
unless you can see.
Time was never on my side
for you to understand me.

Forgive

People find it hard
to forgive others
for common mistakes,
not realizing they're not
cloned with perfection.
If you can't forgive others,
then why should you forgive yourself?
The growth from immaturity,
realizing your mistakes
don't differ from everyone else.
You're forgiving someone
for something you've probably
been forgiven for.
Instead hold a grudge
for an action that's been done before.
The person may have lost your trust,
but they still need your time
to show them those mistakes
can be forgiven with time.
They learn from mistakes,
live through regrets.
The burden of change,
the burden that's left.
Their moment to forget

becomes their moment to remember.
Without both combined,
there's no growth.
Forgiving falls into
a major choice that we make.
Also, remember our choices
make us fall into place.
Your feelings create your plot.
Your heart sets your conclusion.
Should I grip the pain
or instead let go?
Through this experience
there's more to gain.
Pardoning others
will make a difference.
You may change
the falling point
of someone's life in an instant.
People don't ask for you to forget.
They ask for you to forgive.
If you don't,
a normal life they might not live.

it's Never Easy

It's never easy
to make a final decision.

Love isn't blind;
people just dwell with the wrong vision.

Scared to see the truth,
knowing that it hurts.

Your heart may only consume so much
before emotions burst.

Searching for paths to decoy your heart
from suffering and pain.

Giving chance after chance
with the expectation of change.

By now you've brainstormed so much
that you're beginning to think it's you.

Not seeing deep down inside,
you're still trying to escape the truth.

Sooner or later your endurance drains,
the running stops, a decision is made.

Either your heart bears happiness
or it's pierced with a blade.

The person you thought you knew
becomes who you once knew.

The person who stole your heart
leaves you naked with no clues.

Their excuse is they're not ready.
What's holding them up?

Like a volcano, your bloodstream boils,
expands, causing you to erupt.

While your heart remains stable,
the loss becomes your fear.

So, you cuddle yourself in bed
without the choice of sharing tears.

The truth does hurt.
It's not everlasting pain.

Will you make the right decisions
or let your self-confidence drain?

It's never easy.

Why Do Women...?

Why do women
take so long to realize
their vulnerability to wealth of other
men have them captured, lost, into
the greed so stupid. Vagina
loses its value in attempt
to chase
value.
Now polluted,
infected with STDs.
Confused, you should know
what I mean. Too much wealthy penis, not
allowing you to hold yourself clean.
What you portrayed did not matter.
Backfired.
One by one
you left them satisfied.
Too late to ask for respect.
Your temple ruined within minutes.
For greed you sold flesh. Afterward regret. Your
soul, you lost along with it.
Try finding yourself and
conquering your
mind.

While there's
still him, the one you'll
meet in due time, don't let it go to waste.
Maybe it's the one you asked for space
to go chase greed. Seen friends flaunt the fast
life. You couldn't help but need.
Why don't women realize
when the good men
come past?
And when
they finally do,
the time for love has passed.

I'm on My Way

They say I'm on my way
to be a star. That's pretty high.
Picturing myself
in the center of the light
flashing from cameras,
taking my every handsome shot,
upload them to their album,
have their friends say I'm hot.
Or maybe not,
'cause some do hate.
That motivates me more.
Every step on the way
to becoming
the best friend of success.
Being the best at my work,
nothing less.
My aims are high.
My targets are locked.
My accomplishment is near.
Many seem shocked.
They never expect for one
to follow his dreams.
Now I'm on my way
to becoming the theme
of conversations

held at the greatest events.
The success of my name alone
will always represent
the people I've touched
with the work that I've done.
Poetry, my work
that has left many faces stunned,
brought smiles to many hearts,
tears to many faces.
Brought thoughts to many brains,
solved plenty of cases.
Made writing look easy.
It was my life
You, my special friends,
gave me ideas to write.
I looked at your faces
and wrote down your thoughts,
published my book,
the one that you bought.
I dreamed of being loved
every night and day.
You purchased my books.
Now I'm on my way.

Bonus Poem: Bromies

For my special two angels who had a hand in chang-
ing my perspective of love and its innocence through
sibling-hood, Duke and Prince

At the moment, innocence. I have no idea
how or why they are here,
but it's all right
because it doesn't matter.
The joy and laughter shared
melts all the hurt and cares away.
They are teaching us
valuable life lessons,
that we are so distinctively similar.
Yelling "stop" or "mine"—
the "no" or "leave me alone!"
Fighting and wrestling
to prove themselves,
only to realize their natural strength
is in who they are.
And in a matter of seconds
it's back to laughing, playing together,
knowing it's all love.
Don't dare to reprimand one,
because the other will come to a defense.
For they are the only ones

who can make each other cry or fight.
They have each other's backs 365.
Bromies.
Differently similar.
The magic of innocent love.
Brotherly love.
The way it should be even when grown.
But we must take it slow
and go with time because who knows,
they may be the ones
to show how we should be to one another—
you know, world changers.
Friends. Yet blood.
Just pure innocent love.
Yes, they are bromies.

Written by Johaiza De Jesus, the Victorious Warrior

Bonus Poem: Imperfect Perfection

For my daughter, Jaidyn Anaijah. Know you are beautifully perfect the way you are!

Imperfectly perfect,
I have made plenty of mistakes,
causing disappointment to possibly fury.
But he told me he loves me.
Yes, he still loves me anyway.
I'm not perfect. I have caused hurt and pain,
and disappointments, not only to him but also to men.
Yet
he still loves me, He loves me unconditionally.
See, imperfectly perfect.
Every pigment of my skin three tones of brown to
every brown curly strand
of hair that changes with the sun.
Body parts that are bigger than the others, wider than
the others, slimmer,
even prettier than the others.
But he created me, made me, *just like this.*
And he told me he'd love me in *all* ways
always.
Yes, he loves me,
loves *me* unconditionally.

I was created *on purpose and with purpose*
for an assignment to love and heal others
as evidence of his works for his glory,
a warrior for the kingdom yet still a servant to the
Master.
Imperfect, just like this,
wonderfully and beautifully made.
It's not up for debate
that it is the Son shining in me,
which came with a price,
a price that was paid in full.
To live in freedom
with no fear and yet with courage in victory.
Jesus my Redeemer.
Daughter of the almighty and true living God.
Continual praise and worship I will do.
Because of his holiness and worthiness,
I shall praise!
Though I'm not worthy, he kept me,
built for a time like this.
Yes, I was created imperfect.
In and out I am gorgeautiful,
his imperfect masterpiece
of perfection.

Written by Johaiza De Jesus, the Victorious Warrior

Bonus Poem: You

Simple things.
A smile. A word. A touch.
Helping out. Even a look.
It is *you*.
It is the simple things that got me.
Got me to smile. To sit back and reflect.
As my heart and mind processed the alignment,
all my eyes could do was stare and glisten.
It is *you*.
You may never know how much you mean to me.
But that is okay.
For action speaks, and it is saying gratitude.
This formula is nothing complicated.
A simple variable that equals a simple outcome:
love.
The simplest thing, yet so meaningful.
It is *you*.
Loving, protecting, hardworking.
It is *you*. Just being *you*.
Thank you. For the simple yet meaningful
love. Yes, *you*.

Written by Johaiza De Jesus, the Victorious Warrior

About the Author

Jerry Ulysse tackles everyday life in a unique fashion. He's unpredictable but always relatable.